Enlightenment

Finn T. Myles

Enlightenment

Finn T. Myles

To the friends who stood by me through every version of myself, your support made this book possible.

Chapters

Manipura

The Self

Chapter 1

I remember when I was young
figuring out for the first time that the sky was not a picture
I pulled a friend over and said
"Look! You can see the clouds moving!"
They said, "Of course, they do that all the time"
And they ran back to play
I remember watching the clouds move for the rest of recess
and that's when I knew
I was different
and that I understood the earth's language
in a way not everyone could

He doesn't need your dirty looks when he corrects his name
He doesn't need your invasive questions about his anatomy
He doesn't need your jokes about his awareness of who he is
He doesn't need your scowls over which bathroom he feels safe using
He doesn't need your criticism of how he styles his hair
He doesn't need your insults when he carries feminine products
He doesn't need your opinion on how his voice sounds
Most of all, he does not need your approval or permission
to be who he is

A self-made man is no less of a man for the lengths he must go to in
order to break free from society's image of gender

Dear little one, things will get better
There was a reason you liked playing with the boys
Don't let their comments get to you
You know you ran faster
than every single one of them

I'm sorry you couldn't enjoy the holiday
because mom made you wear a
feathered sweater that Easter
I remember your tears as she said
"You look so pretty"
But you didn't want to be pretty
you just wanted to find the eggs
to be happy with the rest of the family

They won't understand
and neither will you, at first
Whenever someone complimented your braids
you wanted to like it but you couldn't
Still, you smiled anyway
Keep that smile going

Don't be upset when your brother gets his hair shorter than yours
there will be a time when you can have your hair just as short
and not be ashamed

Don't worry about the other girls
They won't notice in the locker room
when you sneak into a bathroom stall to change
They may wonder, and so will you
Why can't I embrace my body like the others?
Free to be confident, not hidden
It will all make sense

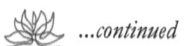 ...continued

You will tell your mom
and she will tell your dad
It's okay to be frustrated when they
don't get your name or pronouns right
Don't expect that to change
Know that your friends and chosen family
will love and support you
hold onto them, don't let go

You will find love
She may be smart, she may be kind
this will be what you need
But some things are beyond your control
She will break your heart, time and again
She will pull away
when you finally understand why you fit in with those boys
why holidays were sad
why you wanted your hair short
why you couldn't live in your skin
know this: it's not your fault

Saving for surgery won't be easy
Those nights, walking late with music blasting
because sleep was unreachable
will end when you take your first look at your new chest
Those countless nights watching videos of people changing
their muscles, hair, voice
will happen to you
if you give your patience and time
It will be worth it
The needles won't hurt that much
though you may cry anyway
You will become independent, strong, and confident
You will love every part of yourself

 ...continued

And just when you think you've found bliss
she will enter your doorway
One more piece will fit
a completion for you and your heart
You will be the happiest you have ever been

So, little one, don't cry
Tomorrow is picture day, and you will have to wear your hair up
Don't blame yourself when they call you names
when your parents ask why you are this way
Get some sleep tonight
Tomorrow will be a better day
Just one more day
until you meet your true self
I can't wait until you do
Because when you arrive
you will understand
why staying alive
was better than dying

I'm afraid, love. I'm afraid
The price of love has yet to be paid
I forever wished for a love like this to exist
but what must I give for life to be like this?

I told myself when I was young
"People live and die when they've fulfilled their purpose
And what if mine
is to find love and leave it all behind?"

I've sinned, love, I have sinned
Where do I begin?
Once fate deems my lungs dry
no one upon my grave shall cry
My skin pale white, my eyes shut tight
Perhaps I deserve to see no more sunlight
only the fire burning my flesh
engraving disgrace upon my chest

I am broken, love, I am broken
watching my step with every word spoken
The love she wrote was contaminated
with guilty, lying lips
leaving my soul naked
on a road so narrow only one could fit
One of us was faithful
one gave up at a hello that wasn't innocent
Abandoned everything
and left me to reason it

I am crazy, love, I am crazy
Reality makes me paranoid and hazy
I've slept next to a vision of my mangled body
hanging in my head among a lobby
of thoughts that never end, flowing down
I answer the voice that makes no sound
rewind the tape of my childhood
show me where I lost it
was I ever good?

Return me to the box from which I once came
You did not ask for this burden, I know
Wrap me up diligently, so there is no blame
Send me off as if nothing was ever meant to grow

Muladhara

The Home

Chapter 2

My father never taught me how to shave
he thought I looked better with makeup

My mother never let me borrow my brother's sandals
she thought I looked better in dresses, in skirts
in the clothes she always bought for me, even though I cried in protest
She said, *"You know, this stuff isn't free? Just put it on*
All the boys will love you
You look so pretty"

My father ignored me the day I cut my hair short
he couldn't stand the sight
My mother never stood up for me
maybe she thought he was right
When I suffered from depression and loneliness
when I begged for an answer and wanted it all to end
they said, *"If only you changed your clothes and your hair*
there would be someone to love you and care"

My father never calls me his son; he thinks I can never be a man
My mother never learned to use my correct name; she never tries
though I know she can

If the human they made is something they can't stand
why bother having children and not accept who I am?
To this day, I am robbed of my childhood, my joy
why can't they find the honesty to finally say

"We would have loved you better if you were born a cis boy"?

You've been wrong about me
from the day I first opened my eyes
and you will be until the day you close yours

Forgiveness is hard
every time you ignore me
What will my opinion of you be
when I stand over your grave
while the preacher's words cross our spirits…

Love. Appreciation. Family.
All things that never applied
I never had a choice

I wonder what your opinion of me will be
as you search for your God
Will you ask me for forgiveness?
What will He think of you
if you never embrace your kin?

It is a messed-up feeling to call someone dad
only to be given a false identity and name
Do you have no shame
in pushing away your only legacy?

Maybe I won't be standing over you
Maybe our spirits won't cross
But I will forgive you
so maybe you can rest in peace

But you will rest alone
You will hear no more of me
What difference does it make
when you already buried my existence?

"What will they say?"
My parents ask me
"What do we call you?"
They will say that I am your son
You can call me by my name

"Please, don't do this to yourself"
they beg
asking me to stuff my soul into the wrong body
They sew my mouth shut with lipstick
so I don't speak of my suffering
They shut my eyes with eyeliner
so I can't see their ignorance
They pierce my ears
with their use of her name
I am not her

I know every week
when the needle hits my skin
that it is worth something
When my classmates call me *"he"*
when the attendance list contains my real name
when my voice deepens
my hair grows
my muscles strengthen
my smile stretches wider
I am myself

Until I am home
then I am stripped of my identity
turned into a persona of gender
written by society
practiced by older generations
enforced upon me
I am not your daughter

 ...continued

I never was

I know these scars across my chest mean more
than the pain they reflect
The surgeon put together more than my skin
removed more than my breasts
Love found me when she kissed those scars
told me I am more of a man
than any man she's ever known
because I fought so hard to become who I am

Every second proving to someone
every expense on drugs, surgery, therapy
She loves me for me
and that's all I ask for

Don't tell me it's hard to get used to
when my friends have respected me
when my brother and sister have adapted
when my six-year-old cousin never questioned it at all

"What will they say?"
I ask my parents
"What do I call you?"
They will say you neglected to accept your child
putting their happiness last

I will not dare call you my parents
You are undeserving of the title
Please, don't make me do this

I may not ever be the
Daughter
Wife
Mother
you wanted me to be
But I can be the best
Son
Husband
Father
that I know I can be and
be happy being myself

Svadhisthana

The Connection

Chapter 3

Sure, there are a lot of things right about me.

But are they right for you?

Now I've come full circle
I've done the impossible
I've redeemed my heart
keeping it in control

Strength never weakens
Anticipation never waits
Pain never enters
where love never hates

I feel dependent
on undetermined prophecies
but I never have flawed attention
to know exactly what they mean

I see you
I hear you
I feel you
Now, dare I say
I want you

My teeth sink into the pleasure of common touch and words
Tell me things about aches I've never heard
Tell me what makes you face the rage of the days
A flavor of possible fear
let me live for the taste

I've never skinned myself bare to dry bone
but the more you steal my layers
the less I feel alone

Forgive me for drifting asleep
amid our late-night conversations
Your voice soothes my thoughts
your touch calms my body

Your energy takes root in my soul
I am trying to listen
but the peace you emanate
leaves me helpless
to this state of spiritual ecstasy

Hold me tightly
Come away with me
We'll meet again in the morning

I've always known
that part of me
let you in and you never left

My thoughts wander
What could be, what is
and now I know for sure
that somehow, the longing meant something

My heart kept making me grasp
lingering opportunities
waiting for me to meet you again
It whispered
"Hold on a little while longer"
until destiny intertwined us
leading us through heartbreak
overcoming manipulation, control, and loss
only to bring us knowledge
in our timed moments
a promise that it will never occur again

Now I lay here
my arms touching your surface
seeing you laugh and smile
things I'll never tire of seeing

We compare fingerprints
hands grazing hands
to the songs of our past
We study expressions
give breath to touch
as I cross my lips lightly against your soul
releasing memories and creating them
feeling your words
in the creases of my skin
I sense you in my veins
I am never more certain
I've always known

I want you to know I love you
and not just hear those words I say so often

Feel them as they roll off my tongue
Let them sink into you

The air you breathe
is the air I love
The earth you touch
is the earth I love
The skin you wear
is the skin I love
The mind you use
is the mind I love

Every space, every measurement
everything that makes up you
are the things I love

The lyrics you scream in the car
the papers you turn when you read
the shows you binge on
I love them all
They bring me closer to you
They expose your bones

I love to see you in raw emotion
because I love the chemicals
that react in your head
Your power of wisdom
your color of sight
your gift of compassion
your sense of empathy
these are all the things I love

 ...continued

Your habits, your daily rituals
sleeping a certain way
cleaning with care
being an amazing mother
dedication to being your best
these are what I love about you

I love you
everything about you
in every way possible

I can feel the essence of your soul
the waves of your love
pulsating through thick air
traveling miles
There's so much to find
in the heartbeats pounding to my ear
as I lay on your chest
I can feel it when you look at me
in the way your lips move
when you speak
I've never felt so much empathy
and endearment in one's very being
The energy you release
is absolute peace

Just when I think things are right
they're not

There's a code you speak
that I am blind to

You have motivation in your soul
to better lives other than your own
to release the burden of caring for yourself
onto your lover

I am trying to love you
as you should love yourself

You say you're independent
yet I see a life not fulfilling your needs
You let it pass by
I see you fading

I saw a light in you
flickering, dying out
Refuel it
Only you can
And I know you can

I Need Some Sleep Tonight

I pray that I find some peace of mind
Peace of mind
The
pieces
of
my
mind

I pray that I can take it back in time
Back in time
Back in time
Bring
it
to
the
back of my mind

I pray that I can believe I am fine
I am fine
I am fine
I tell myself
a
lie
every
time

Help me leave it all behind
Leave it all behind
Help me
I can't
leave
it
all
behind

As soon as I saw contemplation
a look of hesitation
I thought to myself

Please
love me enough to stay, to fight

I know there are problems
some unique to us
some everyone knows, but...

Please
love me enough
Love me at all

So that all we've done matters
and we don't become strangers

Silent Sirens Sleep
tripping uncertainty
They steal the vital things
and don't look back
when they leave

Sirens Awake Sleep
opening up
severed souls from bodies
They speak words of inefficiency
but make sounds like melodies

Even with tears rolling down your face
you were so beautiful
You looked away
thoughts translating through the gloss in your eyes
In a moment, we could slip
in a moment, we could lie
just to keep things together
I felt your leg caress mine
The light from the candle shook and sparked
as though it knew what your skin felt like
Your time is worth so much
I won't waste a second
Your hopes and dreams
are worth more than anything
Look into my eyes
Tell me
how could I hurt you
knowing exactly what you want
knowing exactly what I need?

I'm awake again
lying in the dark
denying myself the truth

My head clouds
when it becomes clear
this isn't what I expected
This isn't what I want

I can master the climb
yet I fear the fall
The heart was effortless
but my surroundings are priced

I still watch you sleep in silence
but something shifts
when you speak
of how I could be better

I know those words won't come
It's there in your eyes
I can't be enough for you

I remember I told her my fear of
falling for her
It was late at night
It almost brought me to tears
I knew once I let the last wall down
opened my soul
and let her walk in
I could only trust
I would become helpless
I am on my way down
and I couldn't be more scared
I think I am the only one
that sees I am falling
But I am going somewhere dark
somewhere I can't escape
where my fears become valid
they become real
My heart is getting tired of fighting it
I remember I told myself
be afraid of falling
falling for her

Will the taste of you
be as sweet as your words
or will it linger
like the bitter aftertaste
of your actions?

You'll be great someday.
Why wouldn't you just do it this way?
I only had one drink tonight.
I'm sick of how we always fight.
Your effort feels inauthentic.
I can't believe you said I was toxic.
Why don't you just leave for the weekend?
This isn't what I wanted.
I didn't think you'd want to come too.
I was only thinking of what's best for you.

    - *Words have power*

I loved Sunday mornings
breakfast in bed
as a family
I loved them
until they became tainted
by unspoken quarrels
Until I realized
I was only counting down the hours
you would choose your next drink
over me

Do you want to know the worst thing you can do to someone?

Tell them you love them and then leave them.

Anahata

The Heart

Chapter 4

How unsettling it is to think
while they held us
as they habitually did at night
we thought we were safe
while they were planning on leaving

The earth sustains nurturing souls
like the roots of a sturdy tree
They bind, they trust, they conquer

Was I wrong to think
that'd be you and me?

If I had known
all the things that you've done
I don't think I would have entered
so willingly

I'm tired of exhausting myself with you
And I know you didn't ask me to
but that is why you loved me
because you saw how much I love
and how freeing it was

Give way to my sincerest hold
These days, the walk feels farthest
and staring from a distance
is getting old

I think these waters defy my instincts
the currents have never been so strong
I see his face
and want to come home

You are everywhere I've been
everywhere I am going
I never wanted a dead end

Say I can turn around

Please
say I can come home

You made me feel
like I didn't deserve love
because I had human emotions

Do you remember the nights
when we didn't say a word?
We could speak with our eyes
hear with touch
We had translucent skin
bonded with friction
that pronounced intentions
and secrets buried beneath
our pasts and fears
Because I remember
everything

I want to cleanse my body of you

The image carved in the back of my brain
you staring into my soul with your eyes
I want it to disappear
It never meant what I thought it did anyway

Your fingerprints on my body
are to be washed away, sterilized
No one will ever see those traces
or the tracks you built to a broken heart

Memories of you are shoved in a casket
where my previous killer lays still
closed, locked, awaiting burial

I want your voice to fade
to a sound so dull
not even a scream could penetrate
my newly built barriers to keep you out

Your toxicity invading my veins
will be followed by pill after pill
to rid your sickness from my peace

No words will ring
no touch will be recalled
It never meant what I thought it did anyway
but these scars I will keep
if only to remind myself how they got there

Trusting in someone who insidiously used me
and left me for becoming weak with selflessness
It is a lesson

A warning sign
So I never again have to cleanse myself
of someone like you

Oh, I see
You mean to say
this was all my fault

Well, I call lucidity to the stand
to help you clarify

You mean to say that your drunken nights
the silent treatments
the disregard of effort
your hurtful outbursts
and me being treated as disposable
did not contribute
to the cracks in these walls?

Let the stars be my witness
and this gash on my soul be proof
that your hands are not as clean
as you say they are

Why would she release you
by giving you closure?

She likes you close enough
to see and feel her
and far enough
that she can do as she pleases

She knows you'll stay
right there, waiting

My mind's in prison
but not on trial for any crime
just there to identify
a murderer of wasted time

A witness, a victim, a survivor
Who was the person that did this?

Triggered by sight
I see her through a two-way mirror
Head down, the air changes
Eyes meet
Her face so sweet, smile like a spell
She knows why she is here
but the confession she will never tell

My brain confused
flood gates break my exterior
her hidden motives
make me forget she's a mistake

Her body doesn't fit the crime
Her body doesn't fit the crime
Her body doesn't fit the crime

Just when I told them I couldn't recognize
this entity as my own killer
the mirror cracks
Frost on her side, the cold creeping in
She's trying to get control
slipping up my skin like an IV in my veins

My breath now visible
as much as I am vulnerable
I can't deny it anymore

 ...continued

It's her! It's her!

Take another look
If you don't believe me
look closer
You'll find all the potential she took
power, manipulation, even in silence
She's got my blood on her hands
It's the best thing she wears

Guilty for attempted murder
Guilty for attempted murder
I swear it was her
I swear it was her...

One person's worst fear
is another's freedom

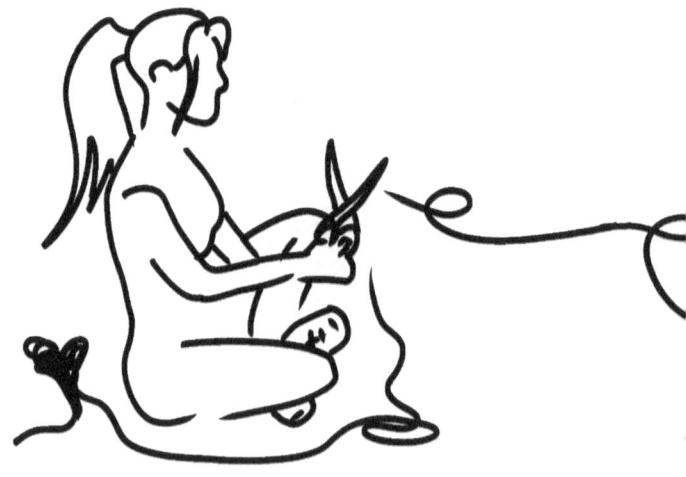

You didn't have to love me...
but you didn't have to destroy me either

I still love you
It's a shame it hurts to admit that
whether I still love
this idea of who I thought you were
or the you that's buried beneath

All that resentment
it's there
I know because I can feel it
though I push and deny
hide and run

I still love you

Go on
Say it to me again
Repeat it
in writing, in sound, in silence

At this point
the ghost of you is forgotten
Acknowledging you? I won't

My body is tired
I was already damaged
the second you tried me on
and I never fit

So go on
Unweave me one string at a time
Do you feel better now?

I find it hard to make sense
of how you questioned my desire for building a family
and tried to use it against me

When it was my love
and my desire for family
that kept me holding on for so long
despite the way you treated me

Let's invest time that will be for nothing
create connections that will haunt us
get so attached it kills us when we're apart

Let's make memories that will have no meaning
keep words written on paper as reminders of what didn't last
blame each other for life's struggles

Let's set distance, get lost and forget where we came from
see all the history and base break
kiss and expose ourselves, ruin ourselves from the inside

Let's talk about the problem but not the solution
start something we can't finish
yell until we just never talk anymore

Let's cover up the good and only see the bad
make ourselves valueless to each other
give up when it becomes hard

Let's not recognize relationships are not effortless
hold impossible expectations of happiness on each other
put our whole heart out there just to break it

Let's let it all fall apart

Maybe I'll never understand
what you want
because you kept it from me
despite my open heart and ears

But let me tell you
what you will never understand
the way you vandalized me
from the inside
walked in, saw how tidy it was
and how I tried to make my heart a home for someone

You were always welcome
Always
Until you recklessly destroyed every bit inside of it
so insidiously, and left because it was an inconvenience
to pick up the disarray

Let me tell you what you won't understand
the shock of seeing it all
trying to put myself back in order
while that same person points all ten fingers at you
and not one at themselves

In the same breath
I want you. I don't.
I love you. I don't.
I miss you. I don't.
I believe in us. I don't.

Breaking the only home within myself
as I hesitantly, yet graciously
gave yours back
without a damn scratch
Let me tell you what you won't understand

 *...continued*

I saw your demons become you
and even with a mess in my body and in my head

I offered you a spot inside
one last time

You won't understand that courage
that selflessness
that pure love

All fingers pointed at me
with fallacious accusations, assumptions, and whispers
only you can see and hear
and in my hands
empathy for you

I will keep my heart to myself
No longer unprotected from you
But I will never punish anyone else for your actions

Next time
that my heart is tidy enough
for company

Walking toward that which I will not tell
not unless you skin yourself as I once did

Talking back, she said
she never knew just what she felt
Let it go because this
will never end

Stalking tasks
Saw figures refining just below the belt
run those heels all over me

Dress it up
Ignore the beacons, wildfires, winter dusk, drought
Reinvigorate these cords
and you will see

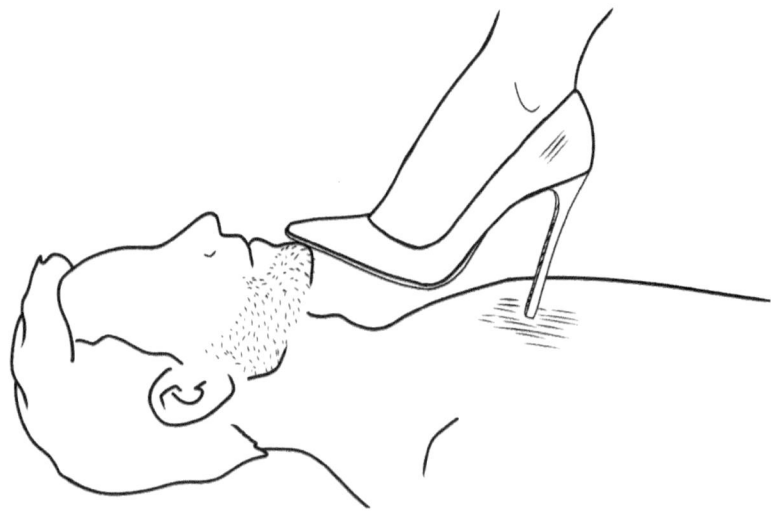

I can only imagine where you are and how you feel
because in reality, I do not know

I don't know if you've ever woken from a dream of me
and thought *how unpleasant*
or how much you miss their touch

I never know when you get that rare text from me
whether you feel reawakened by memories and hope
or bothered by a lingering past

I will never know what you chose to do
with the pieces of myself I left behind
a scrapbook, a note, a small picture

Do they remind you of emotions you wish to ignite again
or ones you wish never to revisit?

I suppose I don't really understand why I still wonder
but I can't help but feel a summer night and think
are you wondering too?

It's taking too long to let go

You knew you didn't love me anymore
but you kissed me anyways

     - *Why?*

Do you know why I was scared to fall in love with you?
For the same reasons you didn't deny that I should have been

I know how I love
I give so much trust
Extending my heart is extending most of me

Why didn't your silence that night tell me something?
Or was it because we were so tightly intertwined?
I was too focused on your lips saying,
"I keep thinking of the L word,"
while you were nervous about admitting you love me

I wonder what that word means to you now
How can it be that you longed for a relationship just like this
with its chemical balance
only to leave?
Tell me, do you miss authenticity?
Because I doubt you will find it so easily
in other people's short-lived storms

It was real for me
I was afraid, and I still am
because the moments I felt peace
were accompanied by the awful truth
I still love you
I still care for you

I couldn't keep giving
You reasons to stay
When you would
Take any excuse to leave

She said she could still feel her energy strongly with me.
I said, I know. I feel her every day, but I don't want to anymore.

- reiki

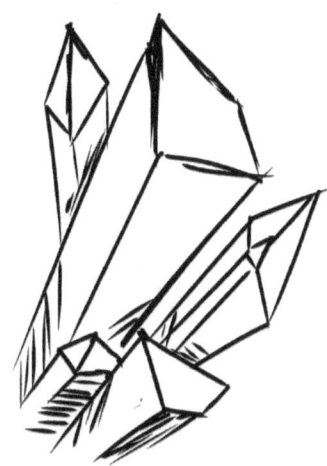

You're going to run out of all your stones
because they will stay right where they landed
Even if they took a piece of me with them
by now I'm sure I can predict
where you will aim next
So why don't you save your stones
for someone who will throw them back?

If she loves you, she wouldn't scream
She would want to spend those nights beside you
see the glow that surrounds you

If she loves you, she would speak of you everywhere
If people know her name, they would know yours too

If she loves you, she would put down the bottle
face the real problems instead of hiding

If she loves you, she wouldn't blame you for her unhappiness
or blame you at all

If she loves you
and truly, deeply loves you
she would be here
talking it out, making it work

You deserve better
Make sure she loves you
before staying in pain one more night

She may think I shut her out
when I said I wouldn't
But the truth is
I was being forced away and isolated
long before I decided
to cut the final ties

All I know is
I will experience love in many ways

But I don't ever want to feel
The darkness she exposed me to
Ever Again

May I embody the strength
to see you for who you really are
and let go of the facade
you weave into reality
that is preserved in my head
and loved with my heart

Ajna

The Intuition

Chapter 5

When things started to become real that's when I saw it
the worry and the paranoia
about me not being honest and me leaving
It turned her happiness into something
not even I could reverse
Every childhood trauma
every unkept promise from her ex
and all of life's complexities
hit her all at once
she looked at me with fear instead of love
and she ran
Oh, she ran so far that not even I
recognized who she was anymore

Maybe,
the moon wasn't saving you
that night

Maybe,
that night it was
saving me
from you

Why do we love the people who hurt us?

Some say it's our lack of self-love, our need for attachment, or perhaps a longing for stability, whether it's financial comfort, resistance to change, or the desire to maintain a perfect image.

But what cripples us to disregard our worth and throw away judgment? No matter how loud the message echoes in our teary eyes or bruised bones, we choose to see a person who loves us, though they may not love us at all.

What makes us low-hanging fruit, so easily persuaded and manipulated by short-lived apologies and long-term reprimands for disobedience? We tremble, trying to stay still in weary waters, to keep the beast near and quiet rather than disturb the pattern by saving ourselves.

What makes us deny this precarious position, trading empathy for a moment of seized abuse? We hold our breath, waiting for a tangible reason to stay, but there is nothing, only the force that shakes the base of the house.

And yet, just when we couldn't feel any more decomposed, their absence dismantles what remains of us. Even when we should begin to heal, we wither and wonder: what could be wrong with us? How do we end up taking all the blame?

I felt cheated
"It happens," you said
You meant falling out of love happens
I agree

But tell me
does it just happen
that the person you should communicate with most
doesn't know where your mind is?

Does it just happen
your lips kissed alcohol late at night instead of me?

Does it just happen
that you invite someone into your home
to meet your son
potentially be a future father
pick him up from daycare, watch him, play with him for hours
feed him, clothe him, teach him
yet never give them a Father's Day card?

Does it just happen
that you express your wants and desires
only to take them back
moments before you break the person
who tried to help?

Does it just happen
you tell that person
"I love you, I believe in us,"
while falling out of love?

It seems like you loved misery more
or maybe just the distractions

 ...continued

Because making someone feel
like they are enough
appreciating them
doesn't start with blaming
followed by avoidance
silence
and hostile reactions to nothing

Falling out of love happens, yes
But this was a crime against my soul

I don't care what you knew or didn't
It doesn't take much to be gentle
to be honest
or to appreciate
the person who would have done anything
to make you happy

Who knows what you look for
in each body you examine with seductive words
and fatal ties

Who knows how much you've taken
from those who are empathetic
and foolishly willing
to let you in

Who knows what will satisfy you
using love as a lure
but the more you seek
the less you find

And we all know
that you're still empty inside

I like how things aren't fixed
This may be in my mind
and it can shape who I am, who I become

It will be there as a memory
but I'm glad that it will fade
become distant

I am grateful for once...

that

     you

         are

            temporary

I remember the first time
I swallowed such a tormenting pill
It tasted like redemption
with a hint of bitterness
but what was worse
was the pain it was distracting from
Her baleful endearments
her vacant apologies
the moments I believed
would never happen again
because of her assurance
And the saying that left my throat so dry
it involuntarily inflicted my senses to suffer
numbed my nerves
It was the sound her lips made
singing like a mockingbird
feeling like Novocaine
keeping me stationary, silent
so what she did
didn't feel like a laceration on my wholehearted flesh
convincing me she was harmless
she dissimulated when she recited
"I love you"

- why I ignored red flags

Loneliness makes me think of better times
and I miss him and having
family, love, and a home
It gives me urges to reach out to you

But there is an illusion here, because
there was toxicity tied to you
and it weakens me to ignore it
Talking to you will not get me anywhere
I cannot find these things I long for
in you anymore

It's freezing in here
The weight of regret is overbearing
When was the last time
someone nurtured this place?
I am six feet deep in sorrow
It soaks through my skin
the smell of a childhood interrupted
by responsibilities that neglected
their own right to exercise love
Unable to accept it
to feel it
to give it
It has the consistency of barbed wire
sewn into innocent flesh
that may or may not still have a living pulse
It is so dark
my sense of sight may as well not exist
for it is a kind of dark
that eats away at reality
the ripples of truth
One cannot even tell
which is evidence
and which is fallacy
But I do not live here
I just chose to be here
I can walk away at any time
I can leave you to this
I don't have to live inside your mind
But you, my dear,
do

- I would have stayed forever but I could never fix you

It was the first moment
that I freed myself from the control of you

I took a shower yesterday
and I felt like I was washing every bit of you off me

It was like meeting myself again
for the first time in a while

I've reclaimed myself
wisdom with it
I feel whole again
but there's always a part of me
that wishes I never had to lose myself
to begin with

I believed you
when you said it wouldn't happen again
I had a feeling but
I thought if I had enough trust
loved just a bit harder
things would change
But what I was really doing
was smiling
while you held my head under water

- We can't love people out of their destructive habits

I know your kind
I don't know what life trauma
made you treat people this way
You tell them they are worth it
but make them work to believe it

You make them promise to never hurt you
then, as they bend to make you happy
you scream bloody murder

You can run from their dedication
which you can't appreciate
You cannot even comprehend why someone would stay
while you shatter their heart
and you bellow out
because you accidentally felt too much
and shattered your own too

I know better than anyone what your kind can do
You break everything you touch

Every morning
I heard her amid my rhythmic dreams
putting on her makeup
asking myself how I got so lucky

Sneaking peeks with my tired eyes
at her beautiful silhouette
in front of the window
surrounded by the sun's glow

And quietly, I waited
because every morning
right before she left
she would come over to me
and kiss my cheek

But one of those times
was not a kiss good morning
it was a kiss goodbye

A Message from My Past Self

I often find myself speaking to my past self
comforting the man who found himself broken
by the loss of family and love
dissolving into a couch
that was never as warm
as the love he gave
but not as cold as the person
who once held him at night

I tell him he will be okay
because that is what I am now
If only I could really hold him
lift his face from the river of manipulation
he was so willing to drown in
touch his heart with real love
and help him see his worth
what he had been wasting

I'd open his eyes to the real person
who leeched off his every positive motive
his vibrant light
his ever-dedicated affection and empathy

It wasn't until recently
I heard him speak to me
from the echoing past
from the depth of temptation
My heart falls so easily
back into darkness
only to try to find light in others

He was disappointed in me
when he witnessed my thoughts

 ...continued

I disgraced every ache he ever felt
everything I ever tried to console
all because of a subtle hint of weakness

He reminded me to be strong
that this is not to be repeated
because we don't want those who destroy others
We are better
We deserve to be valued

I thanked him for this
tour of memories
and the slight pinch of reality

He faded back into the past of my hardships
ones that have been a lesson to me
to better myself, for myself

This wasn't just some love
No, I believed it was the stars
Maybe I heard them wrong

I woke many times aching
a hole in me I couldn't stand
I wanted it to be over
but not to forget, not to give up hope

I tried keeping your energy safe
at the expense of myself
to save you
You never asked me to
I just loved you and him so much

Some days feel like going against the grain
intuition and chance are hard to decipher
I just truly hope you are happy
and one day, my higher self will not wander

It's hard when you choose to watch and not speak
But if you must
I can bear that quiet hold

All we can do is follow
where we feel we must go
I respect what resides in you
telling you that leaving was right

It amazes me
how many faces the moon sees at night
and how little attention we serve the moon

It saw us
between the shades of our room
where we traded our troubles for touch

It spoke to me
the day I left your doorway
and thanked the stars that I met you

It witnessed
all the passing nights we spent going back and forth, arguing
And it heard
every word and silent pause
some longer than others

But even in distance and time
it still sees both of our faces every night
even though we haven't seen each other's in a while

There are nights I am jealous of its light
and so I ask it to wish you sweet dreams for me
I trust that it will
every time

Time has given me the knowledge
that we are from different worlds
What love sustains me
is not what drives you forward
Touch and binding are sacred
where it is just motion to you
Words that cross your lips
are not honest to action
You do not follow through
feel, or give the way I do

I don't know
how you can run your fingers
across my skin
say those words to me
and ignite warmth
create a song
then leave it all behind

Strength? Maybe
Lack of heart? I don't know

All I can really say is
maybe things meant
more to me
than they ever did to you

Belongings
the objects that I have
I dont waste any of my things
I use them until they are broken

and it occurred to me that
some people see others
as objects that they have
belongings

They use me until I am broken

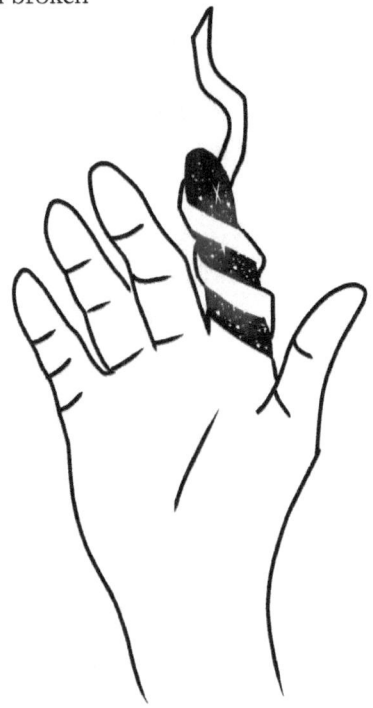

I am a firm believer in action and worth
If they want to talk to you, they will
If they want to be with you, they'll make the effort
If they really love you, they will show you
And anything less than that is not worth
Your time and energy

I still have a piece of your soul here with me
It still lives, breathes energy
in the space you once filled

I wonder if you can feel that
the way I still nurture the thought
the essence of your being

But like a little bug trapped in a jar
it wants to leave
to go where it belongs

I know, for both our sakes
I should let it go

Vishuddha

The Truth

Chapter 6

There's a voice of a child
that runs to me in my dreams
calling for me to stay
asking why I never came back

I'm fighting to be heard
from what feels like
a different universe
with my exhausted lungs I say
"I am so sorry,
I never wanted it to be like this,
I would have never chosen to leave."

Even though he may be
20 minutes from where I am
I'm still accepting that
I will never see him again
He will never hear me

A vivid vision
lights on a tree
Two names positioned meticulously
but a space in between
where another name was placed
an unraveled bell
a memory you tried to erase

Did he ask you
why I wasn't there?
Because during Christmas
I felt none of this was fair

What did you feel
unwrapping those three bells?
Three names that once rang soundly
with feelings you will never tell

I used to hate Country music
but it was his favorite
I listened to it with him all the time

I would see him screaming the lyrics
in my rear-view mirror while I drove
and sing along while jumping
from couch cushion to cushion
I even made him his own CD
so he could listen to it on repeat

I used to hate country music
and now all I can think when I hear it is

unconditional love

I don't think they will ever stop
the thoughts of him that find their way to me
I know it's out of my hands
I know much time has passed
but I still miss him

He has no blame
He didn't do anything wrong
It was neither his choice nor mine

I can't just tell myself to forget him
He still has my heart
I still love the moments we shared
I can't and won't choose to forget that

So all I can do is move on with my life
carry the memories
and be grateful for them

But I don't think they will ever stop

A young one, dull knife in hand
creating a face, tracing a line
challenging the unknown
a nervous man making him laugh for the first time

Crisp air, a sting of cold
Tears on a face
tiny hands shoveling hope
a path of footprints, big and small
a memory too rooted to cope

Dodge a dart, build a track
time meets a disassembled mark
A clean room
a clock to bed
and in the day, it restarts

Work unafraid, a solid bond
he wished to see him grow
But wounds insisted from his past
he had to let him go

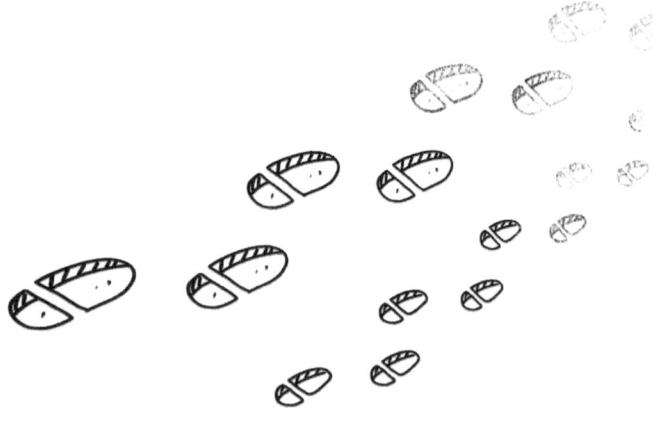

I can still hear him asking, "Why?"
in a confused tone
as I put the AC we all shared in my trunk

she said she didn't need it anymore
but she never told me that she didn't tell him
I had to leave
It wasn't until I was packed and gone
she told him I left for school
I know he knows better than that

I can still feel him tugging on my shirt
pulling me towards his playroom
to show me all his new things
wanting me to stay
I stared down at him
missing him already

There is repetition in my head
That question
how do I tell him that I would stay forever
but it's not my choice
and how can I make sure he knows
even though I have to leave
my heart is there with him
Always

Once upon a time
I was scared that I would turn out to be like my father

I told her how I'm not sure what kind of father I will be
but I know the father that I don't want to be

he taught me more than anyone
that I am better than how I was raised and treated

he taught me more than anyone
that I am nothing like my father

No one ever tells you about the pain of losing a child who was never yours to begin with.

Taking on the responsibility was never a hard choice for me, and neither was letting him into my heart. But the connection we built was never grounded in certainty. Even though I was practically a stepdad, I had no control. Even though I was trying to build a family, there was no security.

I had no choice in being left behind. I have no right to stay in his life, though I long to. It isn't even my place to know how he's doing. When I am told, it feels like mere courtesy, even after all the time I spent with him. Learning about him. Loving him. Spending holidays with him. Feeding him. Dressing him. Teaching him.

I taught him how to swim. On Father's Day, I spent hours in the pool, going back and forth with him. Encouraging him to kick as hard as he could, to move his arms, to stay afloat. Letting him go and watching him succeed. Praising him for a job well done. By the end of that day, he swam on his own. I taught him how to swim… and yet not a trace of him remains in my life. All I feel now is this loss.

It's so hard because he was never really mine.
Yet I told her I felt like he was. I loved him like he was.

I still love him. I still miss him.

And I hope every day that he doesn't think I abandoned him, because I didn't.

It wasn't me who chose this.

As much as it hurts
that he may have forgotten about me
I am thankful to see he is okay
and that this isn't affecting him in a bad way

Even though I wish I saw him
under different circumstances
I am grateful to see
he is growing, he is happy
and he is still the amazing soul
I used to know

Sahasrara

The Stillness

Chapter 7

I take space and break this cord gently
sending my love as you go
I hope it travels safely
as I breathe you out
and disassemble the pieces
of you within me
I appreciate this past
now you should fade gracefully

- Often the hardest, but most necessary

You can and will love again
    You can and will receive love again
        love that blends with your soul

It's true
we can love people who hurt us

And yes
you're strong, to keep on loving, to keep on fighting

But darling
who are you trying to save?

They're already gone

   - When they are no longer the person you fell in love with

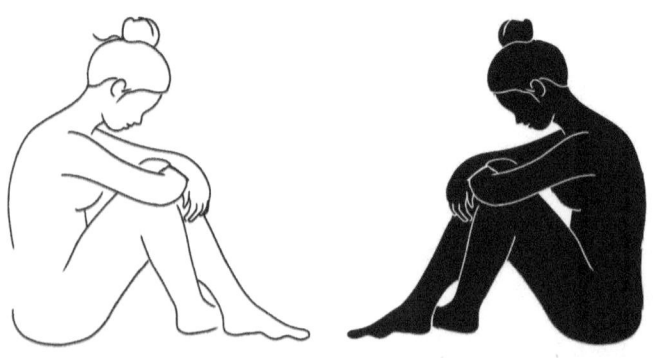

While the world may stop turning
for a second to see you spin
open your eyes to see clearly
the environment you've been in

People's true intentions lie in their actions
people don't want to face reality
They tell you things they want to believe
things they think you want to hear
So when words and actions
don't speak the same language
listen closely to what they do
You'll understand much more this way
words are speculation
actions are evidence

I remember a summer of constant touch
the next summer, a skin-crawling depression
I learned that it took only a moment for me to fall in love
but a year and a half to finally let it all go

How silly it is to realize
that my grief lasted longer than the actual relationship

I recall someone once telling me
that I feel with everything that I am
and I embrace the way in which I give my all

It has to be handled carefully

Gratitude is the antidote to resentment
If we continue to feed the anger
it will soon become bigger than us
What we must challenge ourselves to do
is reflect on what we have learned
how we can grow and harvest
positive energy from this person
or situation
It is not about what we have lost
it is about what we have gained

They aren't the person you first met
but that makes sense

The surface is a lure
their true nature will find its way out

We deserve steady hands
holding the most fragile, vital parts of us

We deserve lust born from over-pouring love
not the use of our bodies for temporary relief

We deserve appreciation and patience
not a leech on our confidence
a hidden thief

My faults are what make me human
my flaws are what make me rugged
Have no doubt, I will bloom
I will flourish even in a fallacious season
without your nourishment
Oblivious as I sprout
you will be absent
as I thrive

I used to look at the one I love
and think to myself
you're too good for me
I don't deserve you

Spending time with myself
meeting parts of me
inviting them to come out
has changed my mindset

Anyone would be lucky to have me

Let it be the last time
you think of them that way
the way they could do no wrong
the way they were perfect
the way they made you feel
the way you loved them
Let it be the last time
if only for acceptance and peace

At some point
words won't matter

Two different vibrations won't match
not unless one changes for the other

Maybe once upon a time
you both were synchronized

but not **anymore**

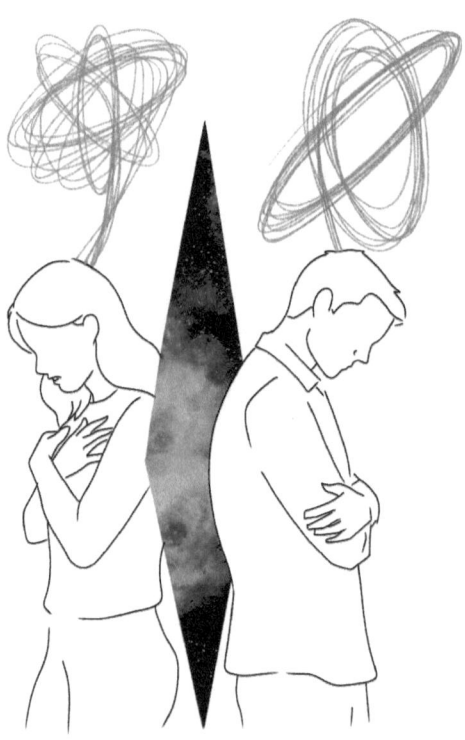

We are all small pieces in this big world
Among it all is us, our purpose
and within our purpose, our journey
our struggles, our progress

Think of the universe
Think of all your grief, fear, regret
all that stops you from moving forward
It is small compared to the bigger picture
yet necessary for you to overcome

Breathe it all in
all the good, all the bad
and wish the negativity safe travels
because you are leaving it behind
and moving on

Breathe out

I carry around these stones in my heart
some are heavier than others
some like feathers but enormous
some small but the weight of a tower
Each day, I let go of the ones that bring me down
and give care to the ones that fill space
and bring me balance

I carry these stones in my heart
some are worth more than others

Destructive people will always have self-destructive tendencies
It is not because of you
You just got too close
You were caught in the crossfire
That is why you got hurt

- It's not your fault

I think we've all had someone
begin to abandon us emotionally
long before they decide to leave physically
The body lingers out of habit
but the heart has already gone quiet

It's okay
I tried making a house
out of ashes
I guess some things
can't be undone

Life is too short
to keep thinking
about what we could be doing
Just do it
Embrace the change, the risk
Feel the pain, the happiness
that's how we live

They can blame it on life
work
time
school

They can blame it on differences
family
hobbies
opinions

They can blame it on anything, really
but I blame them
their lack of
effort
communication
understanding

Because I tried
and they made a decision

I will hold them to that decision

At the end of it all
I depend on myself
I live for myself

Bodies. Broken bodies
Touched by love unkind
Blame the innocent
Watch the self unwind
Before they know it
they're trading truth for borrowed time
just because they can't
leave them behind

- Love is not a contract to stay
Have the strength to walk away
when someone is no longer good for you

You can't find
A remedy for your loneliness
In someone
and call it love

They will tell you they love you
then turn around and hurt you

Sometimes those words
are more about control
than genuine emotion

I am worth so much
I don't have to prove myself
or my capabilities to anyone

I know what I can do
It doesn't matter what other people think
People don't owe me anything
life sure doesn't owe me

But I owe it to myself
to be better, to try
to accomplish and succeed
to fall and get the fuck up again

It's crazy to think
we spend so much time trying to get to know others
If we don't take moments to look within
we could go a lifetime without ever truly knowing ourselves

You can't help those who don't want to be helped
You can't love those who don't want to be loved
You can only move forward

Give where it is accepted
appreciated
embraced
and returned

I keep telling myself I am worthy of love
What I offer may be different, but it is not less
The marks and scars on my body are a story
not a low-quality tag
I am just as good as any other man
My changes have not made me a burden
my journey has strengthened my character
I once mistook uniqueness for inconvenience
I am not a defect
I am my own soul

It's okay to relapse
to cry for them a week later
a month later
a year later...

Let yourself feel it
Ride the waves of emotion
then wait for the tides to calm
and send them away

I wanted her to come back to me
to prove everything she ever told me
to be true

But if anything, now I know
that my fears were valid
and I truly was taken advantage of

If anything, now I've learned
not everyone means what they say
and this wasn't all my fault

I couldn't have saved a relationship
by myself
and I shouldn't ever have to

Sift through people

When mixed together
it is hard to tell what you'll come by
Those who have no will to stay
or no value for you
will fall through

Let them

Those who remain by the end of the process
are the true find
the real treasures of your life
What you're left with will be
pure love and friendship

I feel like I have shed into a new light
I can see my luminance was happiness
in the beginning of you
but it has no comparison to the light
that I have drawn out of myself
It is authentically me
original and self-sufficient
It is my pure energy
and not one conjured by false belief

Surround yourself with good vibes
and if you can't seem to find them
Create and be the good vibes

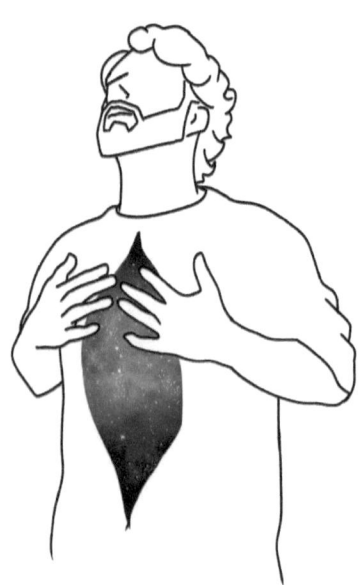

It is a mistake to look for someone to heal you
expecting that with their company
your insecurities will disappear
or that with their love
they will resolve

It isn't true that mending
is the responsibility of your lover
They may appreciate your vulnerability
acknowledge your flaws
understand your weakness
but people cannot heal what only you can touch

You must do that on your own

We must detach our ego
from judgment
See who we love
without predisposition
Release them from
our paranoia, fear, and pride
Leave the past in the past
Love is not about power or control
It is about letting go and trusting
Learn from the past
but do not carry it with you

Don't love me for my body
Don't even love me for how I make you feel

Love me for my soul
because that will be the only constant thing:

before time

in life

and after death

Staying positive is not about smiling through pain or struggle
It is about releasing yourself to the power of the universe
and believing that things are exactly the way they are supposed to be
even if it's not the way you want them to be

The Earth has plans for us all
and we can either fight them or embrace them
Trust that it will take you where you need to be

- Inner peace

If not for what was
There would not be what is

We are forever growing; at no point do we stop
We cannot expect the people we love to be a finished product
They will make mistakes, and they will have many flaws and quirks

But if you find someone with the consistency
of love, effort, and support
that's what you hold onto

I know sometimes
it feels like our hearts are
not meant for this earth

It can be harsh and cruel
and we feel
every fragment
every loss
and every strife

I know we may stumble
and may try to leave this earth
earlier than was meant to be
but trust me when I say
the earth needs hearts like ours

We create
balance and hope
and we manifest
enough love for all

Everyone's just trying to do their best
even if that's not what it feels like
People can be destructive, even in
self-preservation

You

shouldn't

blame

yourself

if

you

had

no

power

to

change

anything

Shift your vibrations
Become emotionally aware
Study your senses

Allow yourself to feel
listen to your soul
notice yourself

Acknowledge what does not strengthen you
and let it go

Appreciate what welcomes you
and let the positive energies connect

What you send out into the universe
comes back

Look at me
See all that I am
vulnerable in front of you
open as can be
This is me

Before you say those words
know that I'm not perfect
and I never will be
I do not live to cross off
a list of your wants and desires
I have my own
I do not seek to complete you
fix you, make you whole
I am doing that for myself

But that does not mean
we can't grow together
support each other
lend parts where the other lacks
owe in limitless love
cherish each other's spirits
and feed the fires of our souls
challenge each other
overcome issues
praise accomplishments
explore new values and opinions

Before you say those words
know that this is love to me
and this is how I will love you
So say it if you mean it
and if not,
say nothing at all

Why do we need
other people
to acknowledge
how great we are?

Just because
people don't see
your worth
doesn't mean
it does not exist

I'm still learning
I must go forward knowing
I will fail many times
but I will obtain the knowledge
that forges the self I will become

I'm still grasping
that even if I am flawless
I can still lose
and in loss
I can still win

The energy the earth expends
will better serve my purpose
whether a lesson or an achievement

I am that much closer

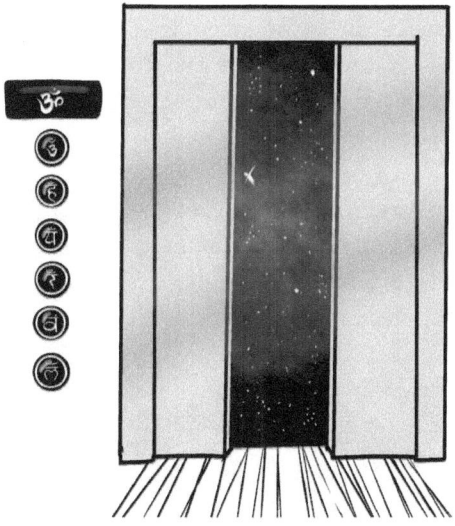

This cold stings
Peeling back my skin
yet numbing all my senses

The night is supposed to be quiet, but it is never silent
Life streams through its essence; it screams in its light
The breath of each soul softly sleeping
and yet your eyes are awake
exposing yourself to the moon

The stars are aligning; they speak only for you
My path is shifting
but I am exactly where I need to be

I have longed for so long
I am afraid to hold
that which I have worked for
yet certain it is molded
for only my grasp

The universe already knows my fate
but considers that which I have asked
It intertwines my destiny with my soul's desire
creating balance

My fingertips are overwhelmed with sensation
reaching, feeling, but never quite there
When will it reach my heart?
When will it satisfy my mind?

The cold slips away
as spiritual ecstasy embraces me
I trust this course

Law of science:
energy can neither be created
nor destroyed
it can only transform
from one form to another

Law of life:
love can neither be created
nor destroyed
it can only transform
from one form to another

If you lose someone
love will always exist
but you will find it
in many forms:
self-love
the quiet peace the earth offers
or blossoming into a new love
a new someone
who gives and receives
love's gentle energy

May you find peace
in the way you
act
speak
and love

I will not accept
anything less than pure intentions and honest love

I will not settle
for convenience in emotion or action
compromising my purpose and worth

I will not give in
to my demons who stagnate me
and dull my inner light

I will
be the love and light I deserve
giving and receiving it in return

I will
keep my boundaries broad but my mind open
attracting that which I seek naturally

I will
learn from my traumas
lay them to rest
and shine my brightest self today

- My Mantra

I hope we are healthier
to those who love us next

Let's hope we treat them
better than we treated each other

In life
you will have multiple destinations
So stop and enjoy this one while it lasts
but always move forward

I do wish you happiness
I hope that you are peaceful
that your life is filled with abundance
and love in many forms

I know things may be different now
but you and I both know
my heart is not capable of harboring bitterness or hate

Maybe when we are born, we are scattered everywhere
our predestined path already seeded with parts of ourselves
Along the way, we gather them as we grow
each experience guiding another piece home

In loss, we find courage
In hurt, we find strength
In lessons, we find knowing
We find ourselves in things, in places, in people

Perhaps when every fragment is gathered
death becomes the highest **enlightenment**
we feel everything
we see everything
we know everything

A Note from the Author

This collection grew over the course of three years, a reflection of my own journey through moving on, healing, and discovering self-worth. Each poem marks a step toward understanding and growth, both in life and within myself.

I'm a small-town author from Massachusetts, and this book was self-published. Independent authors like me grow through word of mouth and reader support. If my work has spoken to you, the kindest way to help elevate its visibility is by leaving a review. You can also share your thoughts on social media to help others discover it. Every post and recommendation makes a big difference.

Thank you for being part of this journey with me.

- Finn T. Myles

Enlightenment

Finn T. Myles